CADENCE

WICK POETRY CHAPBOOK SERIES FIVE
Catherine Wing, Editor

Poppy Seeds · Allison Davis

Here Both Sweeter · Daniel Carter

I Left My Wings on a Chair · Karen Schubert

Determinant · Alex Fabrizio

Local Fauna · Brian Brodeur

Little Nest · Diana Lueptow

Seven Boxes for the Country After · Janet McAdams

Punctum: · Lesley Jenike

Cadence · Hannah Stephenson

CADENCE

Poems by Hannah Stephenson

The Kent State University Press
Kent, Ohio

Ohio Arts Council
A STATE AGENCY
THAT SUPPORTS PUBLIC
PROGRAMS IN THE ARTS

The Wick Poetry Series is sponsored in part by the Wick Poetry Center at Kent State University.

Cataloging information for this title is available at the Library of Congress.

for Henson

CONTENTS

ACKNOWLEDGMENTS

Earlier versions of "Novices" and "Rocker" appear in *UCity Review.* "Nesting" and "Dream Feed" appear in *sidereal magazine.* "Dandelion" appears in *Gold Wake Live.* My thanks to these publications!

"Theorems and Proofs" draws from the classic book, *I Am a Bunny* (written by Ole Risom, illustrated by Richard Scarry, and originally published in 1963). It is one of the most perfect and poetic children's books, in my view, and was also my favorite growing up.

I am so grateful to everyone at the Wick Poetry Center for their support of these poems. Enormous thanks to Catherine Wing for her generous, essential edits and guidance. Thank you to my friends and family for their unwavering love and support. Thank you to Marcus, who challenges and inspires me to be braver and more open; I am grateful for such a loving husband, parenting partner, and dada to Henson. And thank you to my darling Henson, without whom these poems could not exist.

BIKINI SEASON

Oh how much of the world's darkness comes
from shame I mean I want to calculate it with you
At least half And all of us possess a jagged self-splinter
a hangnail a nurtured thorn to drive deep into skin
and suck One very poisonous thought
if I show my soft skin then who will be left to love me
A protected underbelly leads to back and shoulder pain
Leads to loathing of one's core When this pregnancy
was confirmed the doctor said I would gain 25 to 35 pounds
and those numbers and the scale made me wince
Not since my deprivation era had I been subjected
to such frequent weigh-ins Have you ever played a video
of women fiercely smiling in jewel-toned spandex and stood
before them in your living room squatting standing squatting
while the ringleader smile-shouts *Think of bikini season ladies*
Think of it It's coming The one in the back echoes *Short shorts*
sound good right about now The curtains and the blinds all closed
to spare the neighbors of your movements furtive and unnatural
Have you punished yourself enough today Have you held a regret
parade Have you found fault with the alive body that has moved
all day long all your life long Have you hated the body
you were brought to this planet in You were once
someone's summoned darling and swaddled in a cape
with joy emblazoned across it in blue and red
Together let us try to remember we crash-landed in a field
and what waited for us was love

SWAP PLACES

Whoever's dreamscape this is please speak up
and claim it or I'll assume it's reaching out
for my hand Lake that is beautiful who
do you belong to Green-tressed hills do
you have a parent to collect you Every lovely
place feels like it has called me and now I
am picking it up from school Mother wheeling
from home to fetch it All of this is what I
imagine when really it's the land who must
see me as the infant barely here in any
experience So few-seasons-wise to feel
wise Baby within me now I know your name
because your dad and I chose it
and when the snow comes you'll be here
One day we will swap places honey
It will be you who is out here
in the grass which hauls itself up above
the ground as it always has and it'll be me
who is not here Please don't feel afraid my son
This is nothing more than leapfrog

CADENCE

If language could pass through the placenta
what words would I want you to have
If I could give you images what would I feed to you
tenderly

This morning circling water I pass a man on a bench
with two German shepherds beneath him
one old and one young and the next bench I pass
says *Sit with me and be still Maggie* on a silver plaque

and I imagine that someone must have dedicated this to his dog
and I feel guilty for passing you
a picture of a dead dog

A slim teenage girl runs past me
in a billowing tank top It reads *Made By God*

Two-pounder who is still growing in me
Little matter gatherer Ball of yarn that knits itself
Little time recorder Big new stopwatch

What will you do to my cadence when you
arrive

I have you to thank for all this extra blood
in my body

NESTING

From nothing a form What makes a home
A table in the entryway raising its head
under your palm to take your keys
when you walk in Sweet and loyal furniture
Increasingly the local expresses itself to me
with deepening sweetness but oh the farther
away rooms of this country and world hold trauma
What does it mean to hold strangers
in my prayers In the kindest room
of my mind I think unhelpful thoughts
like *I hope the wounded heal* and *May the children
return to their parents* though I know that
some will not Auden handled death by cradling
its horror and absurdity Today I come back
to his words when Yeats died *Far from his illness
The wolves ran on through the evergreen forests
. . . But for him it was his last afternoon as himself*
God this gets to me
Son you are about to inch your way from me
out into all of the worlds that this place is
Already you are yourself When you are born
the deer and foxes will run between the trees
elsewhere in Ohio elsewhere on our planet
Yes the wolves too They race through forests
that feel vast and whole even as we encroach
upon them They look up through tree limbs
and always see sky or just brush past the coarse pines
so very green so reassuringly green

SAGITTARIUS

Horoscope for my son not yet born

This is the sign you will be
I hear you are the explorer sign I hear you
are half-human half-animal although right now
you gallop in place because you are still dreaming
yourself into being Or maybe you are the dream
My body the sleeper You are the unleashed arrow
of the zodiac Baby you will be blunt
This week you are the size of a squash
and so in vogue On every menu squash this
and pumpkin that This week little horse you may
flip and prop your feet up on the headboard
of my ribs As the month ends you will
be ready to finish and ship a professional project
Baby when you are born you will be so unprofessional
thank God This is the week we paint your room
and I've ordered stars to introduce you to the sky
Meteors will come this week but the clouds
will keep them from us Sunburnt rocks will stream over
and although we cannot see them we will know
they are there There is nowhere I can read about you
to learn who you will be

YOU WERE EARLY

In Canada where we used to live sweetie
there is a store called Future Shop
I imagined aisles and aisles offering vignettes
of how a life could look Here is an ocean
for you to walk alongside Here a house in winter
making its own weather Lit-up kitchen against
the blue evening outside Steam over a pot on the stove
Already in the two weeks that you have been here
we have learned about time from you We have lived
all twenty-four hours of some days You dear are time incarnate
When the contractions began I timed and noted them
on my phone And then I stopped observing them
from the outside in and could only be in the middle of them
Your dad and I looked at you to see when you were hungry
and when you ate we wrote it down and made it historical
Soon we will weigh you to see how many ounces
you have swallowed to build your own body
Now there is no future that does not include you
Rearranger of the self I thought I was Reconfigurer of all
that is to come Welcome

DREAM FEED

To eat as the clouds eat
and in eating water become air and cloud

To ingest all that is good

To guzzle sleep to gulp it down

To walk in the darkness toward the back
of the cave and never reach an end

To rock and be rocked
and become a river licking stones
to melt them

To speak into your mouth
a prayer for your voice to grow

To let the tiny dream in you
steep and expand

To be nourished without waking

To take without selfishness
what you need

To drink as a tunnel drinks

To feed and fill your cupboards
while below us along the street the porch lights
croon and croon

To call the light in

NOVICES

Dark road Dark swath of sky visible behind scraggly
darker trees Here we are in the car going home
as I realize we will never be younger than this
Son your clothes are pocket-sized Are marked nb for newborn
That's how large you are Present and born but new
You fashioned us into parents so all three of us are novices
My prayer for myself in helping you forward
toward months is Let me be nimble Let me be dextrous
I have seen mothers manage the props and machinery
before them with one hand and with ease I will get
even better I say it to you as a promise but it is my wish
By the time I can germlessly maneuver you
from car to gas station restroom changing table
you will be sturdier and moving Already your newborn
onesies are tight They stretch to keep you in their grip
a slippery fish squirming within a pelican's bill
I guess the new rule is whatever we master we must
leave behind I guess the new rule is we never master
much and I guess this rule is older than trees Old
as the seeds the stars came from

THIS IS SNOW

I show you snow
because the larger world drops snow today
but in saying it I become conjurer
and guide I name what falls to help you learn
the sounds of our world our snowglobe
Lately every poem I write has the word *world*
in it I once thought that speaking to a child
was small But I know now it is a macro act
This is snow When you hear it again may the sounds
easily find your mind sure-footed and without work
As snow blankets each crevice of the trees
and hedges again and again calling each one
home As my gaze falls over your features
so automatically now Here is your nose
Here is the wall of your plumcheek
When I look at you I tell you about weather
Perhaps I can prepare you for this place
This is snow This is sleet Speaking of precipitation
I drink your tears I don't but it's what we say to you
when you finally produce real tears with your cries
as if true sadness takes a few weeks to kick in
In your oilsheen eyes water readies itself
and within you you are building so many campsites
Here is fear Here is sadness Here is love and comfort
Here is snow You will remember none of these
moments But lodged in you will be I hope
the belief that there are at least two people
who hate whatever even considers hurting you
and also within you names of the weather
which is one way that the world whispers to us

LULLABY

The monster is misunderstood
The monster is left behind
Here are the pearls gritted in the jaws
of the songs and stories I love
and invite into the warm rooms
of your dreams Most often I sing
Puff the Magic Dragon the saddest
song that refuses to end happily
Over and over I listen to myself telling you
how Puff is forgotten and slinks back to his cave
It's awful As a child I loved songs that made me
cry As an adult I am not so different
The Water Is Wide is the other song I give you
Before you were born this was my morning song
as I drove off to teach with you in my belly
dozing beneath the steering wheel
In that song the only monster is water
and distance and time and how they threaten
to fray or bedraggle all our loves
I invite a dragon and a neverending river
into your lullaby so that they can
become your friends I will take their claws
As I sing the boat I am calling for rises up
around us and now I command every dark
and enormous thing Weeping dragons
in their echoing caverns Eddying waters
and the hungers that make them churn
Let them roar We will not fear them
Son in the depths of any monster
we see loneliness As I have on my side
take up your paddle to row And monsters here
grab a paddle or swim alongside us
Dear I will never ever leave this boat

ROCKER

Fatigue hangs so easily from your face
making of your lower lids heavy hammocks
And then when you wake ta da
Smooth pond New sheet pressed and pulled taut
along a pillowtop
This scares me How fragile you are How
lightly you are here but how solid you feel
in my arms
Each day you are more here More of you is in you
As you sleep your self rises within your body
There are things you like and things you do not
Nakedness is good Sweet potato is
good New houses
are bad for two minutes and then they are
good Your nursery is good Your crib is bad
if you startle while I lower you into it
Its slotted rails will keep you as ribs protect
their heart You the heart I lift
and carry against my body to the crib
in the dark The heart I practice putting down
placing into your own bed
Every night I pace with you into sleep
Sometimes I am half-asleep or whole-asleep
in the rocker
These are the unmoored times This is time
with its leash loose and flapping This is the earth
stripped of its seasons
Spring rushing into summer but today
through the window snow
by which I mean the meandering thoughts
of the neighbor's cottonwood What month is it
becoming child What day
Who will you be tomorrow When will I care again
about who I become It's not that I am purely unselfish
honey I sometimes long
for horizontal sleep But for now all I know
how to talk about is you

THE NEW OATH

If a child is in pain, let us help that child.
If a child is in our vicinity, let us not harm that child.
If a child is black. A boy. Neither. Let us help that child.
If a child is at the bus stop
leaving childhood for teenagerdom
or a toddler in a backseat, let us not harm that child.
If a child shares our citizenship or does not.
If a child has done wrong, let us help that child.
If a child is playing with his sister, let us not harm that child.
If a child has behaved like a child, let us help that child.
If a child is pretending to be an adult,
let us not harm that child
and if a human is helpless before us, let us
remember how easily broken or harmed
they are, let us remember the baby they were
as their parents gathered them up in their arms, let us remember
the children they love or might go on to love
if we shield them if we guide them.
Let us remember we are made of
slender bone and stretched, soft flesh.
If if if. When when when.
Amen.

SMASH CAKE

When you wake up how are you changed
little boy What ropes and pulleys are now joined
in your mind and swaying For each new ability
a new rung on your inner monkey bars Your voice
which comes spilling out of your smile Your small
smile And later your grin The anemones that your hands
become fingers curling in and blooming out
How must it feel when suddenly movement or sensations
are available to you An unfamiliar room you find yourself in
that you yourself are building This is why children
love blocks Love tinker toys Love joining two hard bits
to make a changed third thing Baby if you will build
I will bake you the warm bricks and hand them to you
like cupcakes Bang the world's pieces together sweetie
Slam your eyelashes up and down Let your drawbridge mouth
release horns and horses and mandolin-strumming balladeers
who will never hold a sword

DANDELION

In your voice light has two syllables
and a Hebrew gurgle stuffed in the middle
Light is the right noun Little lantern
Little candle Little lumen Little human
Little glowworm Little starbulb
Oh ye of the pearly eyelid sheen
of the luminous apricot face
of the asleep-clasping-me-hand
of the feather curls quilled at your collar
I will paint your portrait
using words you can say
cat light star duck
teeth dog shhh brush hair
brush teeth blue lion
The yell in yellow The awe in rock
The color and light by which to adore it
Tipped bucket of language
You point and say that
Yes honey That
That tree That pink flower That bottle
That mama's hair Avalanche of things
and your mind and mouth chasing them
and my hand and pen scuttling after
New words each day Your newest favorite
You point and request more
More music More water
More dandelions when the stems
clamped in your hand turn to limp twine
We walk and sing Yellow flower
Yellow flower Where could you be
Yellow flower closing like a hand
and then blossoming again as ash
that disintegrates when we touch it or exhale
Star shredded down to its green soul
Light that shushes into snow
into charred match memory
This happens because here in the light
we breathe

STILL CRYING

While my baby naps
I invent five babies to save
   I allow my body to be riddled with bullets
   I kick in a wall
   I wrench a manhole cover from the ground and toss it
   like a frisbee
   I hurtle over a railing
   I brandish a fireplace poker
because I see a video clip of a now-gone soldier
digging through the collapsed universe
of a fallen building

to expose the soft top of a baby's head

who he pulls out while the baby is crying crying
blissfully still crying

May we all become reachers-through-ruin
to pluck out those who need to be saved
May we all become cradles
to shelter them

One day, you'll wish for this back

> is what every mother she knows passes along to her, their voices pinched with clothespins clinging onto sheets that balloon and billow and jerk.

How will I get through this time

> Because it will end. As will the ember of all that you experience, your very ability to experience in and of itself.

The day she comes home from the hospital

> full of bruises and stitches, she stubs her toe on the changing table. It surprises her, that this hurts a little, like before she was a mother.

She didn't remember remembering that song

> but while kissing her son's toes, she starts singing, *Kookaburra sits in the old gum tree* . . . This is how we know that music and time are made of fishhooks.

The baby sleeps two hours this afternoon

> so that inside himself his body can grow. These two hours will not be remembered. He will not look back on them fondly, because he will not look back on them at all.

Naps are lilypads

> for the baby, his brain. He will hop toward who he is becoming, hour by hour.

We cry for the refugees

> only after their children drown. Only after we see the photographs.

I live in a hollow tree

> So says the book that the baby loves. That she thinks he loves. Not for the words, but for their sounds. For the way his mother flutters her fingers over the pages and says *wwwwshhhhh* to make the snow tumble. As the snow tumbles outside.

No one sees any of this

> except the mother. Except the baby. It is unremarkable, but there
> is beauty there. The house grows up around them, a pumpkin, a
> carriage, a hollow tree.

Taking him into the sun

> I learn how strong the light is, how strong the wind is. Mother: a
> shield.

We're going around the block

> and as we pass a thing I share its simplest name. A tree. A pond.
> A bird. A rock. This is my way of giving them to him.

She narrates her own actions

> as she does them, calling herself Mommy before her son. This
> becomes her new habit, casting out a net of language into the
> future to protect her baby, to encourage the world's softness and
> obedience. This is the part of hide-and-seek where the seeker
> calls out to the hider, Ready or not, here we come.

What is the correct pronoun

> for her, for me, for the self. These days, she is more aware of the
> actions of the self, less aware of the self. The girl. The woman.
> The mother. Me.

The streets all end in leaf

> Palmleaf, Littleleaf, and our street, Starleaf. If the streets are
> branches, the houses are leaves. If the streets are leaves, the
> houses are the veins, the palm-creases.

All from love, and no fear

> is what Elie Tahari tells the fashion designers on *Project Runway*.
> I watch episode after episode while he nurses, sleeps, teaches me
> about stillness.

Each day I write a new story

> but each day will also be sewn together in a larger story, and
> each year that book will be sewn between empty covers that
> grow fuller, fuller, fuller. And a shelf awaits. A whole library.

Now it is Saturday

and he sees a magnolia tree and its pink flowers for the first time. Now it is Easter. Now it is Passover. Now it is now, over and over.

The faucet. The pipes in the shower. The window

yawning open. The furnace gulping as it wakes up. The awake birds and the sleeping ones. The whining brakes of the garbage truck. A faraway siren. These are things she mistakes for her baby crying.

A child is killed on a playground

by a police officer the year before her son is born, almost to the day, and the mother thinks often, sorrowfully, furiously, of this boy, of his mother. She puts herself in the scene, in the swings, running to save him. She imagines wrapping herself around the boy, baring her teeth at the officer.

Beauty clutches in its jaws

its opposite. Another way of saying this is that whatever can be ruined is beautiful.

Already with him there are good old days

and there is now. Back when he slept on my shoulder. Back when he was a quieter, more fragile version of himself.

I want him to have the grass

so I lower the car window, so I bring him out into the green world. Together we will inhale the carroty perfume of growing, of tending, of cutting.

Dear Mothers,

What if, with all the love you have for your child, you could love yourself.

Dear Fathers,

What if, with all the gentleness that you offer your baby, you could care for yourself.

One red tulip

at the ankles of the mailbox. Craning its little, lithe neck.

So much of parenting

is having an appreciation for other parents. All of those who
have ever nurtured, one by one, the world's supply of humans.

Like a brass section

a baby's cry reaches out through the screens of the open windows.
Everywhere right now there are infants reluctant to sleep.

Motherhood introduces her to this new guilt

because of all that she cannot do. You are only one body, the
body insists, but the brain and the heart holler out *You could be
doing so much more.*

Here are our bees

she thinks, protective of both the baby and the bees.

For every swath of green

there should be one red thing. Freshly shorn lawn with its
red mower. Red convertible parked under limbs greening up.
Cardinal darting in the leaves of the oak, reminding me that
here is my heart alive inside me for so short a time.

The midday walk brings

purple shutters. A beige house gone blue over the weekend. A
grandfather in black and white checked pajama pants, carrying
his grandson out to collect the mail. They are also in the At
Home During the Day Club.

Stay at home mom,

or housewife, or homemaker. When she considers leaving her
baby for eight hours a day, even for six, her heart sprains its
wrist. But she wrestles with the language of it, these titles that
want to put her inside her home, as if it were a box. Lady in an
aquarium, in a room. Lady inside.

Perry Rules

is shaky-scrawled onto one patch of sidewalk. She imagines a
little boy, Perry, finding the wet concrete, a stick. Hey guys, look,
he's yelling to his friends. Now, the sidewalk starts to digest the
letters, feels itself smoothed by rain and feet over and over again,
an ocean.

Parenthood is a time of boxes

both empty and full. Everything comes to them in a box—high
chair, diapers, wipes, car seat base—and is then unboxed. She
slices them at the seam, flattens them, bodies unfolding into
their own shadows. Or she places them, still folded, inside one
another, nesting dolls.

When her son sleeps in his nursery

for the first time, she feels elation, and then terror. It has already
been six months. There are only six months left before he is one.
And then they only get to have him living with them for 36 units
of six months.

If she could puree the world

to make life easy for her son, she would, but because life won't fit
into the small, be-smiley faced blender, she plops into it chunks
of cooked sweet potato, banana, avocado. From now on he will
eat what grows in the earth rendered thin, fluid, creamy.

Because he has two teeth

up above the pink soil of his gums, she is a little nervous about
nursing. Now he can hurt her. He bites her, smiles and drools,
oblivious. She smiles and laughs with him.

Terrifying headlines about children

mean that she will never read those articles, never. And then she
does, recoiling, wincing, praying.

Trees Are My Business

So says the side of the truck driving through the intersection,
directly across her field of vision. The world becomes their
poem, becomes their book, one street at a time.

This is a story of nouns

Tree. Sky. Bluejay. I point. I carry him closer so he can stroke the leaf. Tree.

The water rises and swells ,

in the tub of her days. The tub widens like a lens, zooming out. Her peripheral vision is returning. Every day they leave the house together.

Remember to take pictures

is what strangers tell her when she is out with the baby. They tell her about their babies, now retired, who have babies who have babies. Eighty-eight years old, husband gone, one son gone, just one son left and all his babies here, family means everything.

In the aisles of Target, a voice: *I am a bunny,*

My name is Nicholas, I live in a hollow tree, the words rising up from some unseen mother's mouth among the red shelves. Her friend the poet tells her this anecdote, saying, *It was like a grand narrator.*

Another name for mother

is the wooden thump of kitchen cabinets opening, closing.

Another word for mother

is the self that makes room for someone else.

Now he resists the stillness

of naps, of solo sleep, of staying on a blanket in the grass, of remaining in one place on the floor. She takes his picture, a blur of turning shoulders, teeth, smile-squeezed eyes, fluffy hair.

It's just like your book,

she tells her son, as they watch the leaves falling from the tree. Down the street, the yellow school bus stops, sighs, extends a red STOP sign, and out climbs a small child. She waves goodbye to the bus, her waiting father waves goodbye, the bus pulls in its sign like an appendage.

The baby is a living bedside photo

> in his video monitor, in his crib. She wakes to watch his back
> raise and lower.

Black bird swooping from one tree to the next,

> tracing a scalloped hem, a bunting. Her eyes follow. In the
> stroller, the baby sleeps.

One red leaf

> in the whole green tree, a mouth. And then, a red leaf at the end of
> every green branch, a blush that spreads. Yellow leaves held aloft
> and mirrored in the gutters of the street. Soon it will be cold.

The smooth birdwing of his scalp

> and its cap of soft hair against my cheek.

Mister Resister

> is what I call him sometimes, pushing against the tray of the
> high chair with his strong legs, straining against the straps of his
> car seat. Baby Hercules. Little big boy.

So many picture books end in *fast asleep*

> and I say it as two distinct words, slowly, intonation rising and
> then falling: Fast. Asleep. The. End. As if the end were relaxing.
> My son, who resists his sleep, knows what I, who resists my
> sleep, know: I don't want to go away.

I curl up in my hollow tree

> *and dream about spring.* This is the ending of the bunny book.
> Curled up bunny in a warm tree, coat hanging on the wall,
> and outside, through the window, snow. Inside the sleeping
> bunny, dreams of all that the bunny has seen—the darting-away
> butterflies and birds, the safest places to hide, the ways the land
> has changed, and everything that will one day bloom, fall, and
> return.